The Birds Come Back

by Mandy Peterson
illustrations by Joe Boddy

H a r c o u r t   B r a c e   &   C o m p a n y

Orlando Atlanta Austin Boston San Francisco Chicago Dallas New York Toronto London

Jack and Mack went on a trip. This time Jack didn't pack too much.

But when the trip was
over, the yaks had to
come back.

Mack had his backpack
and one little bag.

Jack had his backpack,
a box, ten bags, and one
VERY big sack!

A little quack came from
the box. "What is that?"
yelled Mack.

"It's my pet," said Jack.

"I have to have my pet!"

"Do you have to have the sax?" asked Mack. "And the bed, the hats, the pans, the bench, the flag, the sled, the bell, the fan, the net, the map, and the bath mat?"

8

"Yes, I do," said Jack.

"It's all for Gram, Dad, and Mom!"

"What will we do?"
said Mack. "We can't get
it all in a van! We can't
get it all in a truck!"

10

Jack was very sad.
How could the yaks
get back? Then Mack
had a plan.

The yaks went back in a
jet! "What a pal!"
said Jack.